D0990435

DATE DUE

N

SPORTS STARTERS

Slam dunk Basketball

Bobbie Kalman & John Crossingham

Crabtree Publishing Company

www.crabtreebooks.com

Created by Bobbie Kalman

Dedicated by John Crossingham
For John, Danny, Glen and Brad
The street b-ball champs of the Maritimes

Editor-in-Chief
Bobbie Kalman

Writing team
Bobbie Kalman
John Crossingham

Substantive editor
Kelley MacAulay

Project editor
Michael Hodge

Editors
Molly Aloian
Kathryn Smithyman

Photo research
Crystal Foxton

Design
Margaret Amy Salter

Production coordinator
Heather Fitzpatrick

Consultant
Matt Zeysing, Historian and Archivist
Naismith Memorial Basketball Hall of Fame

Illustrations
All illustrations by Trevor Morgan

Photographs
© Sandra Henderson. Image from BigStockPhoto.com: page 23 (top)
Marc Crabtree: pages 8 (left), 9 (left-top and bottom)
Icon SMI: pages 17, 18, 29 (top); JB Autissier/Panoramic/ZUMA Press: page 29 (bottom);
    John Biever: page 21; Darryl Dennis: pages 10, 14, 27 (top); Jerry Lara/San Antonio
    Express-News/ZUMA Press: page 13; Jeff Lewis: page 20; John McDonough: page 16;
    Manny Millan/SI: page 27 (bottom); Edward A. Ornelas/San Antonio Express-News/
    ZUMA Press: page 19; Michael Pimentel: page 22; Gary Rothstein: page 15; Robert Seale:
    page 5; Thomas B. Shea: page 1; Max Turner: page 28; ZUMA Press: page 26
iStockphoto.com: Kirk Strickland: page 23 (bottom)
© Photosport.com: front cover, pages 9 (right), 11 (left), 24-25
© ShutterStock.com: Nir Keidar: page 11 (right); Larry St. Pierre: page 12
Other images by Corbis, Digital Stock, and Photodisc

Library and Archives Canada Cataloguing in Publication

Kalman, Bobbie, 1947-
   Slam dunk basketball / Bobbie Kalman & John Crossingham.

(Sports starters)
Includes index.
ISBN 978-0-7787-3139-9 (bound)
ISBN 978-0-7787-3171-9 (pbk.)

   1. Basketball--Juvenile literature. I. Crossingham, John, 1974-
II. Title. III. Series: Sports starters (St. Catharines, Ont.)

GV885.1.K34 2007   j796.32   C2007-900584-5

Library of Congress Cataloging-in-Publication Data

Kalman, Bobbie.
   Slam dunk basketball / Bobbie Kalman & John Crossingham.
      p. cm. -- (Sports starters)
   Includes index.
   ISBN-13: 978-0-7787-3139-9 (rlb)
   ISBN-10: 0-7787-3139-1 (rlb)
   ISBN-13: 978-0-7787-3171-9 (pb)
   ISBN-10: 0-7787-3171-5 (pb)
   1. Basketball--Juvenile literature. I. Crossingham, John, 1974- II. Title. III. Series.

GV885.1.K34 2007
796.323--dc22

2007002702

Crabtree Publishing Company

www.crabtreebooks.com   1-800-387-7650

Published in Canada
Crabtree Publishing
616 Welland Ave.
St. Catharines, ON
L2M 5V6

Published in the United States
Crabtree Publishing
PMB16A
350 Fifth Ave., Suite 3308
New York, NY 10118

Published in the United Kingdom
Crabtree Publishing
White Cross Mills
High Town, Lancaster
LA1 4XS

Published in Australia
Crabtree Publishing
386 Mt. Alexander Rd.
Ascot Vale (Melbourne)
VIC 3032

Contents

What is basketball?

Basketball is one of the world's most popular **team sports**. In a team sport, two teams play against each other. Basketball teams play on a wooden floor called a **court**. There is a **basket** at each end of the court. A basket is a hoop with a net hanging from it.

*Most **professional** basketball games are 48 minutes long. Each game is divided into four twelve-minute sections called **quarters**.*

Scoring points

Each team has five **players**, or teammates, on the court at a time. During a game, players from each team try to score points. Players score points by throwing a basketball through the other team's basket. The team with the most points at the end of the game is the winner.

Offense or defense?

A basketball team always plays either **offense** or **defense**. A team plays offense when it has the ball and is trying to score points. A team plays defense when it does not have the ball and is trying to stop **opponents** from scoring points. Opponents are players on the other team.

Some basketball players are very tall. Dikembe Mutombo (in white) is seven feet two inches (2.2 m) tall!

On the court

There are lines on a basketball court. The **midcourt line** divides the court in half. **Sidelines** mark the sides of the court. **Baselines** mark the ends of the court.

Doing their jobs

Each player has a **position** on the court. There are five positions. They are the **point guard**, the **shooting guard**, the **small forward**, the **power forward**, and the **center**. Players in each position have different duties to help the team win. Keep reading to learn more about the five positions.

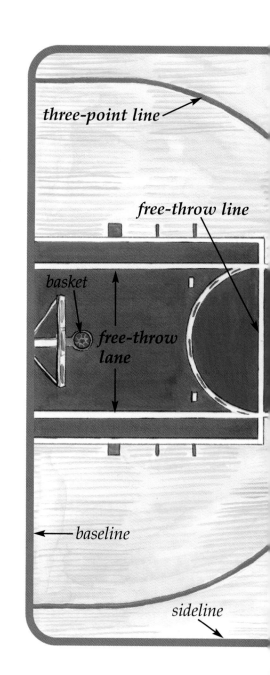

three-point line

free-throw line

basket

free-throw lane

baseline

sideline

In the basket

The baskets are 10 feet (3 m) above the ground. They hang from boards called **backboards**.

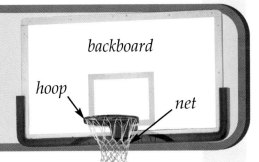

backboard

hoop

net

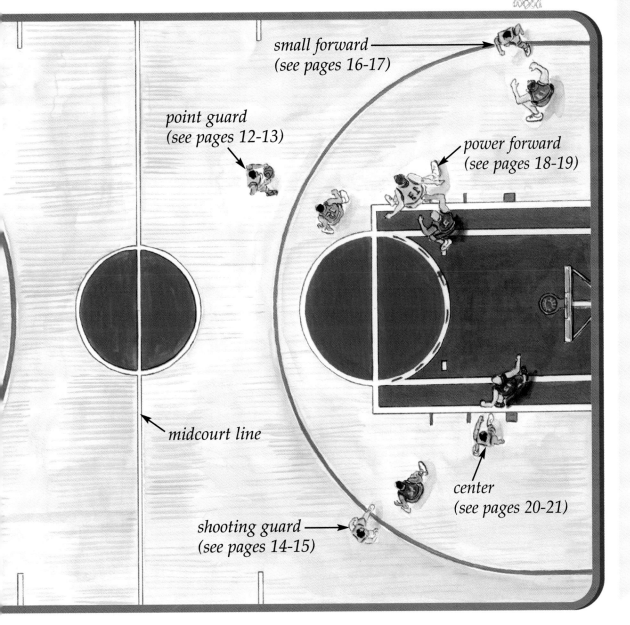

small forward
(see pages 16-17)

point guard
(see pages 12-13)

power forward
(see pages 18-19)

midcourt line

center
(see pages 20-21)

shooting guard
(see pages 14-15)

The way to play

Basketball players use a few basic **moves**, or actions, to play their sport. Some of the most common moves are shown on these pages.

*The player who has the ball must **dribble** while moving around the court. To dribble is to bounce the ball without stopping.*

*To **shoot** is to try to throw the ball through the basket. If the ball goes through the basket, the player scores points.*

When a team is playing defense, each player **guards** an opponent. To guard means to stay close to an opponent to stop him or her from catching passes or shooting the ball.

To move the ball quickly around the court, players **pass** the ball to one another. To pass is to throw the ball to another player.

A **rebound** happens when the ball bounces off the backboard or the hoop. Players from both teams try to grab the rebound as it falls.

Super shooters

There are three main **shots** in basketball. The three main shots are **jump shots**, **lay-ups**, and **dunks**. Players use jump shots when they are shooting far away from the basket. Players use lay-ups and dunks if they are shooting close to the basket.

What it's worth

Most shots in basketball are worth two points. If a player makes a shot from behind the three-point line, the shot is worth three points.

To shoot a jump shot, a player lifts the ball above her head, jumps, and shoots toward the basket.

A player performs a lay-up by leaping up toward the basket and bouncing the ball off the backboard and into the basket.

To perform a dunk, a player jumps toward the basket and throws the ball right through it.

The point guard

The point guard's main job is to get her team playing offense. To get her team playing offense, the point guard dribbles the ball **upcourt**, or toward the opponent's basket.

Get open!
Once the ball is upcourt, the point guard passes it to an **open teammate**. An open teammate is one who is not being closely guarded by an opponent. Once the open teammate has the ball, she tries to score.

The point guard (in red) is dribbling the ball upcourt.

No choice

Opponents sometimes guard a point guard's teammates very closely. When a point guard's teammates are guarded closely, he has no one to pass the ball to. If the point guard cannot pass the ball, he will take a shot.

Built for speed

The point guard is usually the shortest player on the team. Short players can often move more quickly than taller players can. The fast-moving point guard can run around opponents to get the ball upcourt.

Tony Parker has no open teammate to pass the ball to. Instead, he is making a lay-up.

The shooting guard

Sue Bird sometimes plays in the shooting guard position. At other times, she plays as a point guard.

The shooting guard's main job is to take shots from the **perimeter**. The perimeter is the area around the three-point line. The shooting guard runs quickly back and forth along the perimeter to get away from opponents.

Take a shot

Once the shooting guard gets away from opponents, she is open to receive a pass. When the shooting guard receives a pass, she usually takes a shot at the basket.

Short stuff

Making shots from close to the
basket is easier for tall players than
it is for short players. The taller a
player is, the easier it is for the
player to reach the
basket. Shooting
guards are not
the tallest players
on their teams,
so they usually
take shots from
the perimeter.

Dwyane Wade is a shooting guard.
He is taking a shot from the perimeter.

The small forward

The small forward is a tall, quick player who has many jobs on the court. A small forward makes jump shots from the perimeter. He also makes lay-ups and dunks from a spot close to the basket. A team's small forward often scores the most points for the team because he makes shots from many spots on the court.

Shawn Marion is making a dunk.

The best defense

Small forwards are also great **defenders**. Defenders are the players on the team that is playing defense. Small forwards are great defenders because they are quick enough to keep up with, and closely guard, their opponents. Small forwards often have very long arms. They use their long arms to stop passes from one opponent to another.

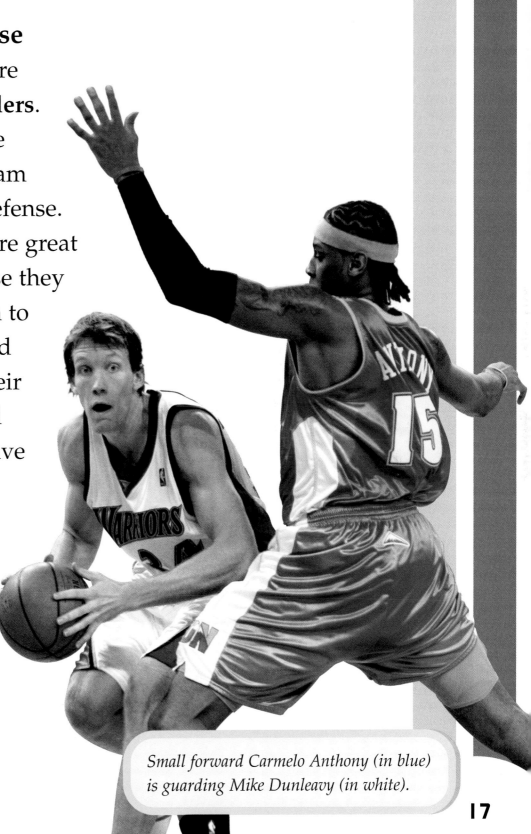

Small forward Carmelo Anthony (in blue) is guarding Mike Dunleavy (in white).

The power forward

Power forwards are tall, strong players. They use their size and strength to **drive to the basket**. A player drives to the basket by dribbling and running straight to the basket. Few players are able to stop a power forward who is driving to the basket.

Chris Bosh (in purple) is a big, strong power forward. Here, he is driving to the basket for a lay-up. Look out!

Tender touch

After driving to the basket, the power forward gently shoots the ball at the basket. If the power forward shoots the ball too hard, it may bounce off the backboard or the basket. When the player shoots gently, the ball rolls easily into the basket. A power forward who makes gentle shots is said to have great **touch**.

Dirk Nowitzki (left) and Tim Duncan (right) are both power forwards. Nowitzki is taking a jump shot after driving to the basket.

The center

The center is usually the tallest player on a basketball team. Many centers are over seven feet (2.1 m) tall! The center does not usually score as many points as the other players do. He helps his team in other ways, however.

Reaching high

The center uses his height and long arms to catch rebounds before his opponents can get them. The center then passes the ball to the point guard so his team can begin playing offense.

Yao Ming (in red) is a center. He is leaping up to get a rebound.

Blocked shots

Centers often use a move called a **block**. When the center's opponents try to shoot the ball, the center makes a block by jumping up toward the basket and knocking away the ball before it goes into the basket.

Dikembe Mutombo (in white) is a center. Here, he is blocking a shot.

The referee

Every basketball game has at least one **referee**. A referee makes sure the players follow the rules of the sport. The most important rule in basketball is that it is a **non-contact sport**. In a non-contact sport, players cannot hit or push one another.

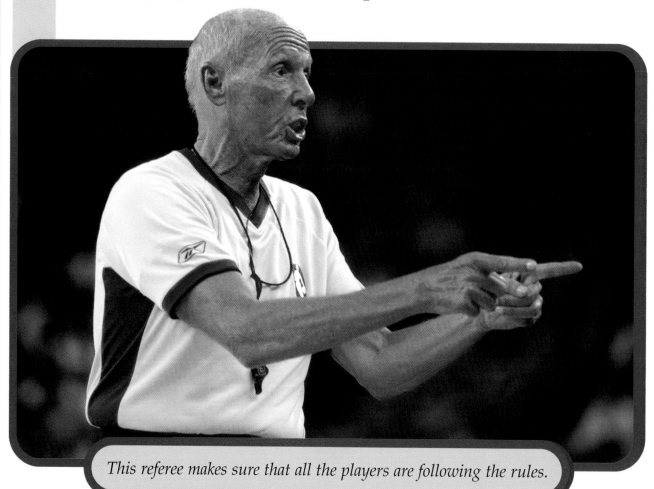

This referee makes sure that all the players are following the rules.

Foul play!

The referees make sure that players do not hit or push other players. When a player hits or pushes an opponent, the referee blows his whistle to stop the game. The player that hit or pushed is given a **foul**. When a player gets six fouls in a game, he or she is kicked out of the game.

The player in black is hitting the player in white. The player in black will get a foul.

Going on a trip

Basketball players must dribble the ball as they run with it. If a player takes more than two steps without dribbling, the player is **traveling**. A player is also traveling if he or she jumps up with the ball and lands without shooting or passing it. When a player travels, the referee stops the game and gives the ball to the other team.

Free throws

When a player is hit or pushed while shooting the ball, she gets to shoot **free throws**. If the shot went into the basket, the team gets two points. The player who was hit or pushed then gets to take one free throw. A free throw is worth one point. If the shot did not go into the basket, the player gets to take two free throws.

Four-point play

If the player was taking a shot from behind the three-point line when the foul happened, she gets to take one free throw if the shot went into the basket. She gets three free throws if the shot did not go into the basket.

24

A player shoots free throws from the free-throw line. While a player is shooting free throws, all the other players must wait outside the free-throw lane.

Basketball leagues

Shaquille O'Neal helped the Miami Heat win the NBA Finals in 2006.

The **National Basketball Association**, or **NBA**, is a basketball **league** that is known around the world. A league is a group of teams that competes against one another. There are 30 teams in the NBA.

The Finals

Each year, the NBA **season** begins in October and ends in June. The season ends when the best two teams compete in the **NBA Finals**. The winner of the NBA Finals becomes the league's **champion**.

WNBA

The **Women's National Basketball Association**, or **WNBA**, is a women's professional basketball league. At the end of each season, the best two teams in the WNBA play in the **WNBA Finals**. Lisa Leslie, shown right, has scored the most points in WNBA history. She has also helped her team win the WNBA Finals twice.

NCAA

College and university players play in the **National Collegiate Athletic Association**, or **NCAA**. The NCAA has leagues both for women and for men. NCAA basketball games are almost as popular with viewers as NBA games are! The best players from the NCAA often become professional players.

Basketball stars

Kids around the world have grown up wanting to play basketball, just as stars Michael Jordan, Larry Bird, and Magic Johnson did. These pages show some of the biggest basketball stars of today.

Tamika Catchings

Tamika Catchings, shown left, is a forward for a team called the Indiana Fever in the WNBA. In her first four seasons in the WNBA, she got the most points, rebounds, **assists**, and **steals** on her team.

Shaquille O'Neal

Shaquille O'Neal, or "Shaq," is one of the greatest centers in basketball's history. O'Neal is over seven feet (2.1 m) tall! He helped his team win the NBA Finals in 2000, 2001, 2002, and 2006.

LeBron James

LeBron James, shown right, is a forward who started playing in the NBA when he was only eighteen. James quickly became a star.

Deanna Nolan

Deanna Nolan plays both point guard and shooting guard for the WNBA's Detroit Shock. She is one of the best players in the WNBA.

Steve Nash

Steve Nash, shown left, is a point guard. Twice, he has been given the **Most Valuable Player**, or **MVP**, award by the NBA. Nash is a great shooter, but he is an even better passer. By passing well, Nash helps his teammates score points.

Time to play!

Basketball is a popular sport for many reasons. It is an exciting sport that anyone can play. It does not matter how tall you are. Anyone can shoot a ball at a basket!

Where to play

Many local parks and schools have free outdoor and indoor courts. So, grab some friends, get on the court, and play some ball!

You can play basketball even without a team. **One-on-one** is a basketball game between two players. It is a lot of fun.

Team play

If you want to challenge yourself, you can join a basketball league. Schools, sports clubs, and summer camps are all places that have leagues for kids of any age. Ask a parent or a teacher for more information about basketball leagues in your area.

Why not get your own basketball net at home? Ask your parents if you can get a basket for your driveway. Playing basketball is good exercise and a great way to spend time with your friends.

Glossary

Note: Boldfaced words that are defined in the text may not appear in the glossary.

assist A pass to a teammate that leads directly to that teammate scoring

champion The team that wins the last group of games of the season

defense The team that does not have the ball and is trying to stop the other team from scoring points

foul A penalty given to a player who hits or pushes another player

free throw A shot taken from the free-throw line after a foul

league A group of teams that plays games mainly against one another

MVP An award given to the best player of the season

NBA Finals The last group of games in the NBA season, to decide the season's champion

offense The team that has the ball and is trying to score points

professional Describing basketball games in which the players are paid to play the sport

season A period of time during which a sport is played

shot An attempt to put a basketball through the basket

steal Taking the ball away from an opponent

touch The ability to shoot the ball softly

WNBA Finals The last group of games in the WNBA season, to decide the season's champion

Index

Printed in the U.S.A.